Your Color Power

Energize, Empower & Enhance Your Life With Color

Other books by Melissa Alvarez

Analyze Your Handwriting
The Writer's Net Anthology of Prose
The Phoenix's Guide To Self Renewal
Paranormal Experiences Volume One
New Age Dimensions Holiday Extravaganza

Writing as Ariana Dupré
Paranormal Romantic Suspense

Night Visions
Talgorian Prophecy
Beneath A Christmas Moon Anthology
Briar Mountain

Featured or quoted in:

Book Marketing A-Z by Francine Silverman
How To Operate A Successful Pizza & Sub Restaurant by Shri Henkel
Successful Meetings by Shri Henkel
Book Marketing 101 by Nikki Leigh

Websites:
www.MelissaA.com
www.APsychicHaven.com

Your Color Power

Energize, Empower & Enhance
Your Life With Color

Melissa Alvarez

Published by

Adrema Press

A NOTICE TO THE READER/LIMIT OF
LIABILITY/DISCLAIMER OF WARRANTY:

The publisher and author have used their best efforts in preparing this book. The ideas, procedures and suggestions contained in this book are the opinion of the author and are not intended as a substitute for psychological counseling or consultation with your physician. All matters regarding your physical and mental health require medical supervision. The publisher and author make no representations or warranties with any implied warranties of merchantability or fitness for a particular purpose. The accuracy and completeness of the information provided herein and the opinions stated herein are not guaranteed or warranted to produce any particular results and the advice and strategies contained herein may not be suitable for every individual. No warranty may be created or extended by sales representatives or written sales material. Neither the publisher nor author shall be liable for any loss of profit or any other commercial or personal damages, including but not limited to special, incidental, consequential, or other damages. There are no warranties which extend beyond the descriptions contained in this paragraph. The publisher and author assume no liability for damage resulting from this book's information.

Adrema Press, P.O. Box 14592, North Palm Beach, FL 33408
Copyright © 2009 by Melissa Alvarez
ISBN: 978-1-59611-070-0

Library of Congress Control Number: 2009905099

First North American Printing: June 2009
10 9 8 7 6 5 4 3 2 1

Contents

The Gift of Color

Have you ever stopped to consider what a gift color is to us on both a physical, mental and spiritual level? What if we could only view the world in black and white as it is with most animals? We'd really miss out on the richness, depth and joy that color brings to our lives.

Color means more to us than just the pigments that we see. As spiritual beings we are made up of color. This display of color is in our aura, our chakras, in our energy levels and throughout our whole system, from the hues and tones of our skin, to our eyes and hair, all of which make us different and unique. Color defines who we are, how we express ourselves and our oneness with the Universe. Color is an essential part of being human and without it our world would be much different.

Just as we are constantly changing in our physical appearance and the colors that we use to express ourselves, we are also constantly changing as we progress along our spiritual paths. We, as spirit, are made up of continually shifting colors dependent upon our vibrational level at any given time. Because of this, we also react to the color and energy vibrations of those around us in different ways.

It's easy to take color for granted because it's such an integral part of our lives. In order to understand the way color can affect us both positively and negatively, we need to look at the meanings of color and the applications of color in order to enable it to work for us instead of against us.

Your mood and sense of well-being can be changed by color—even without you realizing it. Think of the color of the ocean. Its crystal blue with white caps can calm even the severest mood. The pink, purple, orange and golden hues of a sunrise or sunset can touch our spiritual selves. Color affects us in all that we see and do.

There are certain meanings associated with colors because of different belief systems. For example, purple is the color of royalty, royal blue is significant to Christianity, black signifies death while white signifies birth.

We can't discuss color without looking at a quick overview of how we *see* color. Within the electromagnetic spectrum, we're able to see the rays of sunlight within the visible spectrum, which makes up approximately forty percent of the colors contained in sunlight. The other sixty percent is outside our vision and consists of long and short waves. These waves are invisible and include radio waves, infra-red rays, ultraviolet rays, x-rays and gamma waves. It is a belief that if you can open your third eye, you can see beyond the visible spectrum and into the invisible spectrums. Many clairvoyants are able to do this.

The color wheel is made up of primary (red, blue and yellow), secondary (purple, orange and green) and tertiary hues, which are colors achieved by mixing one primary and one secondary color together (red-orange, yellow-green, blue-violet, red-violet, yellow-orange and blue-green). Within tertiary colors there are many specific shades and tints. The layout of the color wheel follows the visible spectrum and makes it easier to utilize different colors to bring harmony and balance to our lives. Using the color wheel can make colors work for you to express your uniqueness.

Color Schemes

Just as the color wheel can help you see the way colors flow in the visible color spectrum, color schemes allow us to put color together in different combinations. This can be used in therapeutic ways. You'll find that many big corporations hire interior designers to create color spaces that will increase productivity in the work place. There are ten basic color schemes.

Achromatic - Uses black, white and grays and does not have color.

Analogous - Uses any three consecutive hues on the color wheel including any of the tints and shades that belong to that hue.

Clash - Created by choosing a color, finding its complementary color on the color wheel, then adding the hues on either side of the complementary color to the original color to create a clashing effect.

Complementary - Uses the direct opposite colors on the color wheel.

Monochromatic - Achieved by using the tints and shades within a hue, including the hue itself.

Neutral - Accomplished by adding black or the complementary color to a hue in order to diminish its effect.

Split Complementary - Created by choosing a color then adding the two colors on either side of its complementary color on the color wheel.

Primary - A combination of the primary colors blue, red and yellow in their purest hue.

Secondary - A combination of the secondary colors of green, violet and orange.

Tertiary - Achieved by mixing one primary and one secondary color together to create red-orange, yellow-green, blue-violet, red-violet, yellow-orange and blue-green.

These color schemes can be used to put together hundreds of different color combinations to be used for a wide range of projects. You can use these combos when you need to redecorate a room, put together a power outfit or even update your makeup. You can create a rich, elegant, romantic, powerful, earthy, friendly, calming, energetic or refreshing appearance, just to name a few.

The Moody Blues

Feelings Invoked by Color

When we discuss the quality of color, which is also referred to as the different aspects of color, what we're looking at is the emotional response that specific colors cause us to feel. This isn't as easy as you may think. We all see color differently. Some people are color blind to particular hues or shades. What I'm sharing here are general observations about color that you can keep in mind while working with different hues and tints. A color that may mean something personal to you could have a more universal meaning to someone else. One color may mean something very specific in one culture but have the total opposite meaning in another. While these are guidelines, always go with what is appropriate for your own culture and beliefs.

If you say red is hot, what you're referring to is red in its fullest saturation. This color grabs the attention because it is very strong. It's quite commonly used in advertising campaigns because it draws attention. Hot colors stimulate the nervous system and can cause aggression. This in turn can raise your blood pressure, make you irritable and agitated. If you have high blood pressure you wouldn't want to sit in a red room for very long.

Instead, you may find a blue room more soothing. The opposite of a hot color is a cold color. Blue in its fullest saturation is a cold color, as is green and blue-green. Cold colors calm you down by slowing your metabolism and creating a sense of tranquility. Think of how you would feel if you were looking at the crystal blue of the ocean in a tropical setting. Even if you're afraid of going into the ocean, the colors will still help to settle a bad mood and calm you down after an argument. Or maybe in this same situation, you go outside, lie under a tree and gaze at the blue sky. It would have the same effect.

The variations on hot and cold colors are warm and cool. A warm color is any color that contains hues of red and cool colors contain hues of blue. What makes warm and cool colors less intense than a hot or cold color is the addition of yellow to the mix. Purple has both blue and red present. Each shade can be considered cool or warm by the amount of saturation of the blue, red and yellow.

Warm colors touch the emotions in a different way. They make us feel spontaneous. They are welcoming colors that seem to embrace and comfort us. Red-orange, orange and yellow-orange are all examples of warm colors. Think back to the beach for a moment and instead of looking at the water look to the sky at dawn or dusk. The sunrise and sunset are examples of warm colors.

Cool colors are green, blue-green and yellow-green. Cool colors give us feelings of renewal and are often found in nature. Think of the trees budding in spring, the way the grass turns from brown to a vivid green as new growth envelopes the land. Spring is a time of renewal in nature and the colors associated with this time of year can also bring about those same feelings in each of us.

Light and pale colors go hand in hand and are in opposition to dark and bright colors. In order to achieve a light color there is an absence of hue. A light color will appear almost transparent whereas a pale color is a soft pastel. Light colors help us to feel rested and pale colors are seen as gentle and they calm us. Dark colors have more black in them and they tend to make things seem smaller (like a room or our waistlines). They tend to be thought of as serious colors, professional and efficient, and can make us feel the same way. Dark colors can also be depressing if they are not complemented with brighter colors that lack the gray and black hues of a dark color. Bright colors grab our attention because they are vivid. It's actually very hard not to notice them. Who would want to ignore them when they give us feelings of excitement and happiness?

Colors within Us

Chakras, Auras and Energy

Chakras

Now that we've gone over the basics of how we see color, different schemes and the aspects of color, how is color a part of us on an internal level? We all have auras (ever-changing life energy surrounding the human body), chakras (seven centers of spiritual energy within the body) and energy levels (varying degrees of high and low energy). Color is associated with each of these areas. Let's first look at color in association with our chakras.

The Crown Chakra is the seventh chakra and it is located at the top of your head. It is associated with white, purple and violet. This chakra connects you to higher realms. It is your ability to "know" and is a key spiritual connection between yourself, the Universe and God. Some consider it to be our connection to the divine, thus the colors associated with this chakra reflect that. Pure white is associated with all things spiritual in most cultures. Purple and violet reflect royalty and heavenliness.

The Third Eye Chakra is the sixth chakra and it's located inside the forehead between your eyes. The color associated with this chakra is indigo. This chakra gives us the ability to see the spiritual realms. It's important in the development of psychic abilities, trusting intuition and seeing into other dimensions. Indigo helps to open your mind to higher realms and enables you to become more sensitive to others and to yourself.

The Throat Chakra is the fifth chakra and its color is blue. It is located in the throat and is important in self-expression. Creativity stems from this chakra. Blue brings insight and wisdom, is key in self-reliance, realizing your own independence and your feelings of responsibility to others and to yourself in life. Blue is associated with our higher selves and is able to soothe and calm us so that our creativity and self-expression can flow smoothly.

The Heart Chakra is the fourth chakra and its color is green. I bet you thought I was going to say red, right? This chakra relates to your ability to give and receive love, forgive yourself and others, and it affects your self-control. It's located in your chest and influences all relationships. Green is a relaxing color that enables us to give and receive love unconditionally. That is why the color for the heart chakra is green and not red. Red is a powerful grounding color and that's why it is important to the base chakra, which also keeps us tethered to this existence.

The Solar Plexus Chakra is the third chakra, the center of our emotions, and its color is yellow. It's located right above the navel. It directly affects our thinking abilities, our personal power, ego, self-confidence and humor. Yellow is also associated with the intellectual part of our brains. The meaning of the chakra and the color assigned to it go hand in hand.

The Sacral Chakra is the second chakra and is sometimes referred to as the Spleen Chakra. It's located right below the navel and its color is orange. It's associated with our ability to feel, to interact in social situations and our feelings during intimacy. It is important to our sexuality and reproductive abilities. Orange frees and releases emotions while lifting your spirits.

The Root/Base Chakra is the first chakra and its color is red. It is located near the tailbone at the base of the spine. It is connected with our ability to survive and it grounds us in the physical world. It holds the eight cells that contain the knowledge of creation. It is a power chakra in that it controls our ability to stand up for ourselves and others, our personal feelings of security and our instinctive nature to survive. Red is a power color. It's strong, hot and draws attention. Red is associated with the root chakra because this color gives us strength through its power. Red works with the root chakra to ground us in this existence instead of allowing our heads to always be in the clouds.

Auras and Energy Patterns

Our auras are also composed of colors. Some people can see auras, others can't. Regardless of whether you can see auras or not, they exist and can even be seen through aura photography. I'm not really good at seeing auras but occasionally I'll see some colors within an aura though they appear as a flash and are easy to miss.

As I practiced trying to see auras I suddenly became able to see a person's energy pattern and colors associated with that energy—but guess what? It was in the wrong place! I was trying to see the aura colors radiating around the person's body but suddenly I saw a river of energy rotating around the person's waist. This first happened when I was doing a reading for a friend. This energy ring is similar to the ring around Saturn, but it has the consistency and flow of water. It has depth, motion, speed and I can see swells and obstacles in the energy patterns. At first the ring was a dark gray and over the course of a year, colors started showing up during the readings. Now this energy ring is filled with colors. I gave up trying to see auras radiating from a person's body because I feel like I am seeing them—just in a different place. Color is a big factor when I do energy readings now and the color meanings are the same as it is for auras.

What do the manifestations of certain colors within an aura or energy pattern mean? In this section I'm going to go over each of the primary colors in the aura and in energy patterns. Each color has a different meaning but you will take into consideration all of the colors and individual shades within a color. If you really want to learn this, it will take time and practice but I believe that you too can learn to read auras even if it shows up in a different place as it did with me. I've also found that once you know what the colors associated with energy patterns and auras mean, you can look at other areas of a person's life that seem to reflect the colors in their energy/auras. The colors they use when decorating their home or in the clothing they wear can give you insight into their energy. Here are the basic meanings of color when reading auras or energy patterns.

Red

People who have a lot of red in their auras are full of life and sexuality. They are passionate, ambitious and sensual. These are usually powerful people who demand attention in both the workplace and in their personal lives. They're all or nothing and give as much as they get. When the aura or energy is dark and/or cloudy it indicates that they're holding in anger and could have violent tendencies.

Pink

When pink is evident in an aura or energy pattern it indicates that the person is a romantic. They are full of ideals and tend to be modest and shy. Their nature is very gentle, loving and caring.

Purple or Violet

These two colors are associated with people who have mystic qualities. They may be very spiritual either in regards to their religion or they may be metaphysically inclined and use psychic abilities to help others. They tend to have high ideals and expect a lot out of the people that they know even if they don't come right out and say so. They look at the bigger picture instead of focusing on the small details. Being around someone with a lot of purple or violet in their energy will make you feel a sense of open-mindedness and great expectations from life. They are people who can make you see possibilities when you thought all of the doors and windows were closed.

Indigo

You'll also find the same sense of inspiration and spirituality around those with indigo in their energy patterns and aura. They seem wise beyond their years and are adept at staying in control of themselves even when they can't control what is happening around them. They are patient with others and sensitive to everything. They usually have an affinity for animals. If indigo is around someone then to them all things are possible.

Blue

This aura/energy color belongs to people with high levels of intelligence who think logically. They tend to be rational in their outlook on life and don't often lose their cool. When the shade of blue is very clear, the person is intuitive and probably has psychic abilities even if they don't actively use them. A dark blue indicates a suspicious nature. Trust is hard for someone with dark blue in their energy/aura and even when trust is earned, the suspicion may remain. Steel/slate blue combined with gray shows a person who is in control and who doesn't like to lose that control. They tend to be very cautious and don't take risks.

Turquoise

Want to talk? Then find someone who has a lot of turquoise in their energy/aura. These people are dynamos, with abundant energy, who can keep your mind spinning with their new ideas and plans. They like to lead and pave the way while bringing you along with them because it's going to be so much fun that you can't possibly miss out. They are organized, efficient and will take charge in any situation. They're usually not overbearing but if you see deep shades of turquoise with a splattering of gray then they can be a little much on the system and you may find you need a break from them. They can make you tired just watching them.

Green

People who have a lot of green in their energy patterns or auras are very balanced and have a deep seated calmness. They have a gentleness about them that others may find soothing. They're kind and caring. While you might want to cry on the shoulders of someone with yellow in their energy/aura, the person who has green will sit you down and have a good heart-to-heart over a cup of coffee or tea. Not only do they have a solid foundation, an even focus and non-shifting balance for themselves, they want you to have it too and they'll help you achieve it. Green is a nature color, it promotes healing and rejuvenation and this person will readily share this with you. In energy that primarily consists of another color but has a twinge or streaks of green this indicates jealousy or a deception. They may not be exactly as they seem and may have devious plans hidden deep inside.

Yellow

This color will appear in the auras and energy of people who are extremely happy, have bubbly outgoing personalities and who radiate joy. These are loving people who are full of compassion. They are free spirits who love life, have good shoulders to cry on and they will cheer you up after you cry. Usually they don't shirk responsibility but if the yellow is dark it can indicate a happy but suspicious nature. They will not take your word for something but will instead double check behind you just to be sure you're telling the truth. When the yellow looks dirty or has specks of brown then this person is hiding a deep pain that may also be accompanied by hidden anger. When dirty yellow is seen, it's an indication that a time bomb is waiting to explode because the hidden energy is in direct contrast with the normal happiness that would surround the person if the pain and anger wasn't there. This person can cover up really well because it's their true nature but eventually the pain and anger will fester and come to the surface.

Orange

With a similar meaning as yellow, orange indicates a person who is outgoing, lively and generous. They'll give you the shirt off their back if they think you need it and take you out to dinner too. They have warm personalities and are quick to make friends. They'll get you out of the doldrums quickly and inspire you to great heights. They can tend to have too much pride if there is a lot of orange in their energy patterns/aura. When streaks of orange are apparent, this indicates that the person can get their feelings hurt over imagined wrongs.

Gold

When a person has a lot of gold in her aura or energy patterns this is showing that she is very spiritual. They are leaders who help to enlighten others so that they can move forward on their own spiritual path. They are mentors and guides here on Earth. Few people have a lot of gold around them, even fewer have only gold. Usually what you'll see are traces of gold, streaks and nuggets scattered throughout their energy. This shows people who are balanced in all areas of their lives. They're good-hearted and helpful without concerning themselves about how their good deeds will affect or come back to them in the end. They do the right thing from a soul level.

Brown

This color is another one that gives warning. The person with brown in her energy/aura is usually in a bad mood and wants you to be in a bad mood too. They have a negative outlook on life and are quick to bring you down when you're feeling happy. If they have to be miserable then so should you. They feel like everyone is out to get them and everything they do will fail. You can't convince them otherwise. Brown indicates that the person can't focus their energy into positive outlets. When you see streaks of brown in a person's energy/aura this is indicative of that person experiencing difficulties in life. Streaks of brown usually pass when the problems are resolved.

Black and White

Seeing black or white in a person's energy is usually a warning sign. These are two colors that you can't really compare the use of the same color in their home or clothing to the energy of their aura. There are plenty of people who don't have black or white in their auras or energy patterns who like to wear or decorate with black and white. When black or white appear in energy/auras this usually indicates substance abuse or illness. Black is also indicative of someone who has emotional problems or they're just downright mean and nasty. Other times black is showing that someone is full of fear and worry. They may have panic attacks or be afraid to leave their homes. Regardless of the problems behind the black or white in someone's energy/aura, it is a clear sign for you to be aware and use caution when dealing with this person.

Gray

This color is also a warning sign and can also indicate illness but not to the extreme that black or white does. The person may be sad and lonely, depressed or anemic. They have low energy levels and tire quickly. Fear may be gripping them and causing their energy to drop even lower. They may be anxious and not like social situations. Some people with gray in their energy/aura are just going through a difficult time and the color will disappear as they get well or change their outlook on life. Others may just have a hard time coping with life in general and gray is a permanent part of their energy/aura.

Opaque Colors

When observing one's aura you'll notice that you'll be able to see through the colors of energy. If you can't, then this is considered an opaque color. It's very dense and light can't get through it so you can't see through it. When you observe a dense color in an aura or energy field, it shows that the person is struggling with something difficult in their lives. They may have unresolved situations that they're trying to work out. This is also a sign of regret.

Transparent or Clear Colors

A transparent or clear color is the opposite of an opaque color because it is easily seen through. Think of looking through tinted glass – the lighter the color the more clear it becomes. When discussing clear colors it doesn't mean they are totally without color but instead the color is easily seen through. When the colors in a person's energy/aura are clear, it is indicative of someone who is an open book. They are usually happy, carefree and don't try to hide behind masks or shields. They tend to be wonderful friends who care deeply for others and are loyal to the end. They look at the positives in life – their glass is always half full and never half empty. If you're feeling sad then a person with clear colors in their aura is sure to lift your spirits.

Now that you have a good idea of what the different colors evident in an energy pattern or aura mean, think about the people around you. Look at their actions, the way they look at the world and how they act and react to situations they're involved in. Can you make an educated guess at the colors that may be present in their energy/aura? I bet you can.

Does this new way of thinking about color in accordance with someone's personality traits help you to understand them better? As you meet new people in your life, look at their use of color, their personality and personal presentation to the world. Using color analysis in this way will give you a keener insight to people on a deeper level. Then, if you're able to view auras or energy patterns (or once you learn), you can see if you were right.

Color can be a powerful tool to aid you in your day-to-day dealings with friends, neighbors, acquaintances and coworkers. You can also use color to change a bad day to a good one, create the image that you want to present to the world, to improve your health and bring balance to your soul.

Feeling and Breathing Color

Did you know you can feel and breathe colors? You may not have considered this possibility in the past but both of these methods are very helpful and healing to us in our everyday lives.

Let's start with feeling color. Did you know that you can feel colors though your hands? Blind people are very much attuned to the different energies of color and they feel them by recognizing their energy though the sense of touch and feeling the color though their skin. Feeling color is done on a more subconscious level but you can learn to do this too by becoming aware of the energy and vibration of each color.

Have you ever had articles of clothing that make you feel warmer or cooler? Some feel comfortable while others make you uncomfortable. Reds can make us feel hotter while blues can cool us. If it's the middle of summer red may not be the color to wear. Instead try blues or greens to cool and soothe you.

Feeling Color Exercise

If you'd like to learn to feel colors by touch, here's an exercise that you can try at home. Buy a book of construction paper or pieces of felt in a variety of colors. Sit down at a table and put the squares of color in front of you. Start with just one or two until you can distinguish between the two colors only by the energy and vibration that you feel.

Close your eyes and hold your hand a couple of inches over each color while tuning into what you're feeling in your hand. Do you feel warmth or coolness? Is the energy vibrating at a fast rate or slow? Let's use red and blue as examples. The red sheet will feel like it has waves of strong, warm energy radiating from it. The vibration will seem to move quickly though your hand. Now hold your hand over the blue. Do you feel a change? The energy will feel cooler and calm. The vibration will feel slower.

Now add two more colors to the mix. If you keep the papers stacked beside you then you can take two sheets from anywhere in the stack and put them in front of you without looking at them. This time, use both hands simultaneously, holding them slightly above the sheets. See if you can distinguish the differences in the energy and vibrations of each sheet. Try to decide in your mind what the colors are in each location. When you have a color firmly set in your mind, take a look. Were you right? If so, add more sheets. If not, practice on these four until you can mix them up and still be able to distinguish between each sample.

Once you learn to identify colors through touch, you'll always have this ability. It's not something that you'll easily forget because the colors will always radiate the same energy in the same vibration. This is a fun exercise to do and it will help you when the power is out and you have to get dressed. That way you'll never be mismatched…even if you have to get dressed in the dark. Of course you could use a flashlight but where's the fun and challenge in that?

Breathing Color Exercise

How can you breathe color? This is achieved through a simple exercise that you can do on your own or you can work with someone else to help them bring balance to their lives by participating in a color breathing session.

The first thing you want to do in this exercise is choose what you need to work on—are you sick, tired, depressed or have a mental fog? For example, if you've got a terrible cold that's just hanging on, then the color you'll choose to help this condition is green. Reference this list of colors and the areas that they will help before you start the color breathing session. There are some medical conditions that I've included in this list so I want to say up front that you should always get checked by your doctor if you're having medical issues. Use color breathing *in addition to* (not instead of) any medical advice that your physician may prescribe to you.

Red

Use this color when you need more energy and/or self- confidence. It's good for any problems related to the circulatory system (tingling and numbness in the arms and legs) and blood. It's also good to use when you're experiencing sexual problems (both in a relationship or with problems in the genital region). If you find that you're often cold, surround yourself with red to warm up. Anemia, arthritis, asthma, low blood pressure, colds, heartburn and night blindness are all issues that can be helped with the color red.

Pink

This color works well on acne and breast problems.

Magenta

Use this color when you are having brain fogginess, trouble concentrating or any other mental problems. It's also a good color to use with heart problems.

Violet

This color is useful when treating arthritis, baldness, bladder problems, gas, rheumatism, scalp problems, tonsillitis, wounds and emotional problems. It also eases the pain of childbirth.

Indigo

Use indigo for allergies, an excessive appetite, croup, dandruff, nosebleeds, migraines, eye problems and skin problems. It is the key color for the nervous system.

Blue

This is another color with a long list and it also interchanges with green. It helps toothaches, anxiety, back problems, blisters, high blood pressure, bronchitis, pneumonia, coughs, palpitations, hiccough, hoarseness, laryngitis, diarrhea, spasms, nausea, nightmares, pain relief, bleeding, burns, skin problems, respiratory problems and rheumatism.

Turquoise

This color is good to heal earaches and throat problems. It acts as an anti-inflammatory color.

Green

You can use green for the same situations as blue, plus anxiety, bleeding, breast lumps, bruises, chicken pox, concussion, cramps, cysts, diarrhea, obsessions, fevers, hay fever, sinusitis, menopause, mumps, strep throat, ulcers, colds and flu.

Yellow

This color has a long list of ailments that it can help. These are abdominal cramps, abscesses, headaches, loss of appetite, excessive burping, constipation, colitis, indigestion, stomach problems, any problem in the kidney, liver or lymphatic system and diabetes.

Orange

If you're feeling sad or depressed then orange can help. It is also a good color to use if you have abdominal pain that may be caused by hernias or kidney stones, muscle aches or spleen problems.

Once you've selected the problem you're going to work on and the color associated with it, the next thing you want to do is a creative visualization exercise. To prepare for this, find a place where you can sit or lie down comfortably and be undisturbed for at least thirty minutes. The key here is to be relaxed, so if it's difficult to find the time during the day without worrying about the phone or any other disturbances then try this exercise before you get out of bed in the morning or before you fall asleep at night.

1. Pace your breathing so that it is in a regular, calm manner. Breathe deeply so that you'll get the most oxygen benefit (but don't go too quickly) by taking one deep breath after another. Just pace yourself with steady, even, deep inhalations and exhalations.

2. Protect yourself by visualizing the pure white light from God and the Universe surrounding you. Let it enter you through the Crown Chakra (top of your head) and fill you completely all the way to the tips of your toes and outward to the tips of your fingers. Let this white light soak right into the marrow of your bones so that there isn't any place in your body where you are not Light.

3. Once you feel that you are totally immersed in white light, protected and prepared, imagine the color you selected coming to you in what may look like a cloud or mist. I usually see a cloud but the form it takes is up to you, as long as it can easily move through you. As this brilliant light filled with your color choice surrounds you, let it move into you in two different ways. Let it be absorbed through your skin and let it enter

through each of your chakras. When you use both the skin and chakras you will gain the most from this exercise. Open the chakras to receive the color energy you are visualizing by imagining energy swirling through them. If you have trouble opening the chakras, start with one at a time. Open the crown chakra during this exercise, the next time open the crown and the third eye chakra. Keep adding another chakra until you're able to allow the color to fill each one and be dispersed throughout the body by the chakra based upon the duties of that chakra in your system.

4. During this color absorption, think of the healing properties of the color as you continue your breathing. Imagine it working through your body, correcting the problem that you've chosen it for, to help you heal. Once you feel that the problem has been corrected and/or the healing process has started, then on each inhalation, imagine the color attaching to all of the negative energy associated with the problem, illness or emotional situation. Sometimes you may have to do this exercise more than once for the same problem until it is finally resolved; it just takes time.

5. Now exhale. As you release the breath allow the color to leave your body, taking all of

the negative energy, toxins, unnecessary emotions and illness with it.

6. Repeat this until all of the color has completely left your body, healing, cleansing and balancing you.

You can do this exercise as often as you like using different colors to work on different areas. You may also use more than one color during a session to work on more than one problem. For example, if you need to work on anemia (red) and strep throat (green) during one session, imagine the color red coming through after the white light and then green after the red. Make sure you wait until the red session is complete before starting the green session. It is also a good idea to send white light throughout your body between colors so that the next color can do its job completely.

Now you know how to *breathe* color.

Colors and Fear

We all have hidden fears that we don't readily admit to others. These fears prevent us from connecting to and being our true spiritual selves. Fear also keeps us from living life to the fullest and meeting our potential. If fear does these things to us then why do we hold onto it? Because we are afraid to release fear. If you truly want to, you can eliminate fear from your life. Will it be hard to do? Yes. Is it worth it? Most definitely.

As I thought about this section I tried to pinpoint both a fear that I've overcome and my biggest fear right now to share with you. My biggest fear is loss—whether it's losing someone I love, loss of income or loss of respect from others. As I thought about this fear, I realized that the fear doesn't stem from contemplating the actual loss but from what would occur in the aftermath of that loss. What would happen to my children if I wasn't here? How would we provide for them if we couldn't work or lost our jobs? Would my peers and readers respect me less if I stumbled over my words or said something incorrectly or didn't know the answer to their question during a public appearance? Looking for and finding the root of your fear is the first step in overcoming it. So take a few minutes and look at your fears—really truly look at them—and write them down. Once you've faced them you can start to eliminate the fear.

Let me tell you about a fear that I've recently overcome, which illustrates how you can use color to help you conquer your fears. I've been doing clairvoyant readings online for years but I'd never really promoted my readings. Instead, I thought that people would find me if I was supposed to read for them. Over the past year or so I kept having recurring dreams of myself in the public eye doing readings on a larger scale. That scared me because these were prophetic dreams and I wasn't ready to move to the next level in regard to my abilities. So I fought it tooth and nail. I ignored it and hoped it would go away and it didn't. One of my psychic friends had been reading the same thing for me for over a year but I was being hard-headed and ignoring her too. Sometimes I have to receive messages multiple times before I truly listen on a soul level. One day, in a casual conversation about clairvoyance, I did a brief reading for someone and a person who I didn't know looked at me and said, "You're strong, you're very strong," and then left the room. I found out later she was clairvoyant too. Now I was being given messages about this from my friends, in my dreams and in my daily life from people I didn't even know. So I finally gave in and decided that I'd be okay if I released my fear of being in the public eye more.

When I got home that day I used the color breathing exercise above to surround myself with red energy. I drew it inside to take away the fear, while leaving me a feeling of energized awareness. I chose red because it is a grounding color and it helps you overcome negativity, which in my case was the negative energy associated with fear. After the exercise I felt energized and ready to accept whatever God had planned for the public presentation of my abilities. If I feel this fear trying to gain a foothold again, I repeat this exercise using blue or green to calm me. Since I've faced this fear I've seen an increase in interest in the readings that I do and in my knowledge of metaphysical topics even though I haven't done anything else differently than I've done in the past. I believe that once you face your fears more doors open up to you. Doors that fear kept shut in the past.

What about the things that we fear in our daily lives? Are you afraid to fly? Or maybe you're afraid to swim, take a train or go to the mall. Whatever your fear is you can overcome this fear by using color.

Let's use flying as an example. Let's say you're afraid of flying but you have to take a flight for a wedding, or business or for whatever reason. You simply cannot get out of boarding that airplane and streaking through the sky, thousands of feet high up in the air sitting in a hollow metal tube with only re-circulated air to breathe. If you're afraid to fly, I bet that description made you cringe, didn't it? That's step one—acknowledge your fear of flying. The next step is to analyze why you're afraid to fly. Is it because you think the plane will drop out of the sky and you'll die? If so, then your fear is really the fear of death and not the fear of flying. Or is it because you hate small enclosed spaces and stale air? Whatever the reason, look at your fear and say "Okay, Fear—I know you're there, holding me back. I don't like how you make me feel so it's time for you to hit the road."

But you still have to take that flight, right? And releasing the fear of flying isn't going to happen overnight even if you've acknowledged it. Here's where color comes in to help you before you take that flight.

1. You'll have to find where the fear is residing within you through creative visualization, using images and thoughts to search through your body to find where the fear lives (see Breathing Color Exercise in previous section). Note, it may just be hiding behind your liver or somewhere else where it'll be hard to find.

2. Now that you know where the fear is inside you, do a color breathing session (or two or three), using calming colors like blue and green.

3. Apply the color directly to where the fear of flying is residing inside you and once it's well saturated, let the color filter through and penetrate your whole body. Applying the color directly to the fear first is like using a bleach stick on a white shirt stain before throwing it into the wash. You work on the spot to remove it before cleansing the whole.

4.   Repeat this exercise until you feel better about stepping on that plane.

As you overcome your fears through acknowledging them and using color to empower and heal that which scares you, new doors and opportunities will open for you.

Power Colors

Essential Essence Spirit Color

Power colors are the true color of your spirit and soul. They are the colors that you feel drawn to and that you use in your daily life. These are the colors you like to wear, use to decorate your house or even like to eat. So let's take a look at how you can determine your essence colors.

Grab a pen and paper. We're going to make a list. I want you to write down the following:

Your favorite color.

The color that relaxes you.

The color that inspires you.

The color that you notice most.

The color that you eat the most.

The color that you wear the most.

The color that you feel protects you.

The color that makes you happy.

The color that gives you strength.

The color that annoys you.

Now take a look at your list. Do you see any colors repeating? If I were to answer these questions my responses would be: Blue, Blue, Red, Green, Red, Green, Gold, Green, Red, Orange. This shows that my three essential essence colors are Blue, Red and Green.

Does your list have ten different colors? This doesn't happen often but if it does find the primary color family. For instance, lilac would belong to the purple family. Once you have your colors down to three then those are your essential essence colors.

Essence colors usually don't change very much during our lifetimes. These colors show us what we have to work with and the obstacles we must overcome. Essence colors reflect your personality. Let's take a look at what each essence color says about your likes, dislikes and character traits.

Red

If you're a red then you're high energy, excitable and like to be the center of attention. You often act on impulse and are fast paced in everything you do. You strive to be the best and sometimes step on other people's toes to achieve your own goals. Reds often have a high sexual desire, are passionate and loyal. They're creative, fun-loving and courageous extroverts. Reds must be careful not to feel victimized by others and situations. It is easy for them to become resentful and impatient, irritated and in a bad mood. If you dislike red then you may have suffered rejections in the past that make you less trusting now. You may feel like everything you begin ends in defeat so why bother? A dislike of red may also be a sign of illness.

Pink

If you're a pink then you're the ultimate affectionate person with a very loving nature. You are a good listener who is understanding and compassionate. While you're great at giving support, you also need more support from others than most colors. You can have your feelings hurt easily when it comes to love and relationships and may even imagine hurts that aren't there. You can lack willpower, which makes you seem weak to some. Pinks do well to use warm colors around them to help improve their self-image. If you dislike pink, this shows that you probably have issues that have never been resolved with your mother or father.

Purple

If you're a purple then you're intuitive, have high standards and ideals, and feel things very deeply. You show concern for all around you but you tend to compare them to your own high standards. For those who don't measure up, you don't bother with them. You can become arrogant and self-serving if you don't find balance within your life and spiritually. If you dislike purple then you may feel that others are holding you back, blocking your creativity or trying to make you conform to their belief system.

Blue

If you're a dark blue then you're responsible, smart and tend to rely on yourself. You feel things deeply and need downtimes full of tranquility, love and tenderness. You're affectionate and like to receive affection in return. You may be a workaholic and tend to carry more than your own weight, which leads to stress. You like quiet; noisy situations grate on your nerves. If you're a light blue you're more sensitive and creative. You have an engaging imaginative streak. You like to work at your own pace. You can be very perceptive and analytical, which allows you to be a good problem solver. If you dislike blue then you're afraid of failure and the loss of status, income and dignity that will accompany said failure. You also could fear someone disappointing you and loss of loyalty from others.

Turquoise

If you're a turquoise then you are sensitive and creative. You draw people to you without trying. Others find you to be invigorating, a source of calmness in their hectic lives. You are fresh and seem innocent even if you're not. You worry too much about others and may do too much to help out. If you dislike turquoise then you're avoiding your feelings, shutting down and getting into a rut because you're afraid of change.

Green

If you're a green then you're an observer of life rather than a participant and don't like to volunteer in events, choosing instead to live quietly and on your own, staying in the background. You're overly cautious and don't trust people. You don't like conflict of any kind and seek stress free situations as often as possible. You're sensitive and like to remain in control of things that directly affect you. You can have a negative attitude and have to work hard to remain positive when things go bad in your life. If you dislike green you may be lonely, afraid of rejection or in a time of grief.

Yellow

If you're a yellow then you're active, like sports or any activity that keeps you moving. You're able to deal with life's challenges, disappointments and conflicts with minimal stress. Yellows tend to be spontaneous and fun loving. They're not afraid to take risks and are idealistic. They are interesting people with lots of friends and acquaintances. If you dislike yellow then you've lost some of your own personal energy, self-esteem or motivation. You've been disappointed and are having a hard time getting past that event.

Orange

If you're an orange then you are active, competitive and action minded. You're impatient and restless. People may often think you have "ants in your pants". You can motivate yourself without being told what needs to be done. You're a strong personality and may be thought of as dominating. Easily frustrated, you need to stay in control of projects because you feel as if you can't count on others to do it right. You're creative, practical and filled with gusto. If you dislike orange then you're exhausted—mentally, physically and/or emotionally.

Gold

If you're a gold person then you live by high ideals. You're dependable and trustworthy. You look for the good in people and radiate power. You're wise and understanding. You have the ability to instill hope and self-belief in others. You're inspiring, lack fear and are self-assured. If you dislike gold then you're rejecting material or spiritual wealth and have self-esteem issues.

Brown

If you're a brown then you're honest, sensuous and protective. You hide your secrets well and seek emotional security. Acceptance by others is of great importance to you and you feel isolated if you're not part of a group. You like being around others and having fun. If you dislike brown then you are in a period of change where you'll strike out on your own more than ever before, you'll change your attitude and this will electrify your energy levels.

Black

If you're a black then you have inner control. You have strong opinions, are very independent and tend to be inflexible in your ideals. You are opinionated and outspoken and like to be in control of everything around you, even to the annoyance of your friends and family. Blacks tend to use the color to hide a lack of confidence or indecisiveness. If you dislike black you do not like to give up power to others.

White

If you're a white then you are well-balanced, optimistic and have positive energy. You're a leader and work at your own speed. People tend to look up to you because you don't follow the rest of the pack but have individual ideals and your own moral code that you live by. If you dislike white then you need to break free from a situation and make key decisions in your life.

Gray

If you're a gray then you're living to the beat of your own drum. You're a person who can take care of herself, who is in control and has good judgment. Grays have to be careful about becoming too passive in their outlook on life so that they don't become isolated and lonely. Grays often need to make time for rest and relaxation because they tend to work too much and play too little. If you dislike gray then you need support from those around you, especially spouses, friends and family.

Once you've determined your color power then refer to yourself as such. I'm a blue, red, orange or whatever your color may be.

Food Colors

Color plays an important part in the foods we eat, the presentation at the table and the way we perceive our meals.

Do you sit down at the table for every meal? Or are you so busy that you often find yourself eating over the kitchen sink? In today's age of fast food and on-the-go dining, more and more people find themselves using the drive-thru and bringing home a quick meal. It seems that the days of cooking and presenting a full-course meal every night has gone the way of the dinosaurs. But this is an extinction that can be reversed if you want to do it.

When you're setting the table for your meal, you want the tableware to be pleasing to the eye and inviting instead of just plain and ordinary. If the tableware color is bland then the impression of the meal will be bland too. So make a change and spice it up a bit. If you normally use plain white plates trimmed in pastel flowers, try solid plates in red, blue or green. Not only will it evoke different feelings about the way the table is set it will also set a different tone for the meal. You can also add color to the meal by adding flowers and greenery as decorations to the food.

Think about this for a minute. Have you ever been to a picnic where white paper plates were used? How about a picnic where red plastic plates were used? I have and boy, what a difference a color makes. In my experience, the picnic with the white plates was fun and entertaining but the picnic with the red plates was kicked up about twelve notches. The same people were in attendance, it was another birthday party, but why was the second party more hyped up than the first? I swear it was those red plates. They were the only thing that was different. Red is a power color that energizes you. When you eat from a red plate, you're getting the benefits of the color red along with the food.

This same principal can apply to any meal. Try using bright-colored plates at breakfast to wake you up and give you energy. Tableware in contrasting colors will offset the color of the food and make them more mouthwatering and appealing. You shouldn't put food in the same color dishes. For example, don't put peas in a green bowl — they get lost and will seem bland. If you served peas in a red or dark blue bowl the color is contrasted and the peas look even more delicious.

The colors of foods themselves should balance out each other. You don't want to have a plate that is filled with all one color. Broiled chicken, white potatoes and rice served on a white plate does not make a colorful meal. Instead go for a rose plate with grilled chicken (with nice black grill lines), corn on the cob and black beans over the rice with some roasted skin-on red potatoes and French cut green beans to the side. This adds a variety of color to the meal, which makes it more appealing.

Some foods are naturally warm or cool based on their colors. Warm foods heat the blood, improve circulation and raise blood pressure. If you have high blood pressure you'll probably want to stay away from eating too many warming foods. They often have a strong or bitter taste. Cooling foods tend to be salty and are associated with white, green, blue and some purples.

Warm foods are asparagus, red peppers, chilies, cayenne, leeks, chives, green onions, ginger, walnuts, roots, chicory, endive, kale, rhubarb, apricots, peaches, cherries, raspberries, guavas and kumquats.

Cool foods would include barley, tofu, whole wheat, buckwheat, millet, kelp, eggplant, mushrooms, water chestnuts, bamboo shoots, cucumbers, lettuce, celery, cauliflower, cabbage, beans and sprouts, pears, blueberries, cranberries, grapefruits, blackberries, bilberries, watermelon, apples, persimmons, bananas, mangos and tangerines.

The exact colors of foods are also beneficial to know when you're planning your meals.

Red Foods

Red foods are considered warming and stimulating. They heat and raise the body's temperature, release epinephrine, increase energy and vitality. They arouse the reproductive areas and make you feel uplifted, confident and willing to take the initiative. Red foods should be eaten when you're cold or if you're anemic. Examples of red foods are beets, cherries, red bell peppers, red meat, watercress and leafy green veggies that contain iron, chilies, rhubarb, red kidney beans, red apples, ginger, raspberries, tomatoes, strawberries and rosemary.

Purple and Violet Foods

Purple and violet foods help the nervous system and mental problems. They act as a diuretic, have sedative properties, are purifying and protective. They are associated with intuition and spiritual understanding. Purple foods have powerful healing effects and are soothing and help to restore a calm peacefulness to our systems. Examples of purple/violet foods are beets, purple onions, purple grapes, eggplant, purple broccoli, purple bell peppers, purple cabbage, lavender, globe artichokes and red onions.

Indigo Foods

Indigo foods have a stabilizing effect. They purify, reduce fears and help to free the mind of inhibitions and fear. Indigo is associated with the pineal gland, which controls nervous, mental and psychic abilities, sight, hearing and help to treat the ears, nose, throat and eyes. Examples of indigo foods are black beans, black olives, black cherries, dried raisins, vanilla beans, wild mushrooms, currants, soy sauce and boysenberries.

Blue Foods

Blue foods help to lower temperature, fight infections and have antiseptic, antifungal and anti-inflammation properties. Blue foods help to still our minds, aid our speech so that we speak clearly and help us in our self-expression. They should be served with brightly colored food or on a colorful plate so that they don't cause depression. Examples of blue foods are blackberries, blueberries, bilberries, mulberries, prunes, kelp, blue plums, garlic and juniper berries.

Green Foods

Green foods are cleansing. They purify and balance us while acting as a stimulant. They help the heart, lower blood pressure and are soothing to the nerves. They relieve stress, help emotional problems and alleviate headaches. Examples of green foods are cucumbers, lettuce, green peppers, zucchini, pears, string beans, green grapes, kiwi, limes, peas, broccoli, peppermint, parsley, cabbage, endive, capers, green apples, celery, artichokes, alfalfa, oregano, tarragon and asparagus.

Yellow Foods

Yellow foods cleanse us and empower our minds. They aid in digestion and help our nervous system. Yellow foods are good for the skin, help to bring balance on an emotional and mental level, stimulate our minds and aid in concentration. They raise our spirits and make us optimistic. Examples of yellow foods are yellow-skinned fruits and veggies, lemons, butternut squash, bananas, nuts, butter, seeds, rice, pineapples, yellow melons, corn and yellow oils.

Orange Foods

Orange foods are warming and give energy and mental stimulation. They aid in digestion and act as an anti-depressant. Examples of orange foods are oranges, carrots, cantaloupe, egg yolk, paprika, ginger, squashes, pumpkins, apricots, mangoes, tangerines, papaya, cumin and guava.

Now that you have a general idea of the types of foods associated with different colors, you can use these foods to bring balance and boost your immune system. When you eat food of a specific color you're boosting the energy associated with that color in the energy systems within the body. When you feel that you're out of balance, use creative visualization (see Breathing Color Exercise) to pinpoint where the imbalance is coming from. Determine which color would best bring you back into balance and then add more of that color in your food. Once you're feeling balanced again, then you can go back to an even distribution of color in your diet.

Color in Your Home and Office

The two places where we spend most of our time are home and work. The colors used in these spaces need to be organized in a way that enables us, regardless of what we're trying to accomplish in a particular room. The rooms should be appealing to the eyes and appropriate to the room's usage. When you're decorating make sure you consider different color schemes, which may be complementary, clashing or calming. These schemes may be hot or cool but as you look at the space as a whole there should be flow from one area to another. Are there specific places in your home or office where one color would work better than another? Let's take a look at the colors used in decorating to find out.

Red, burgundy, wine and brick are warm colors that give their warmth to a room. It gives a rich feeling to space but it can make rooms appear smaller than they really are because of the darkness and depth of color. These colors are excellent in accessories to give just a flavor of warmth but can be overpowering when the room is done up in all red tones. It'll probably make you crazy after a while and then you'll be priming and painting all over again. Try to avoid reds in your bedroom, sunroom, den or, if you're into mechanics or woodworking, in your shop. Reds are great colors for the kitchen and you can find all kinds of appliances in red these days. It's good for any area where you want to increase activity like a kid's play area or your personal workout room. Small areas like hallways, stairs and alcoves are excellent places for red tones.

Pink can be very relaxing, as can rose, shell, salmon and blush. Pink has a nurturing and restful effect, so much so that you may even feel like you've been sedated. This is an excellent color choice for a nursery or preschool-age child's room. It's also a good color choice for an elderly person's bedroom. Actually it's a nice color for all bedrooms. In the office, patient's rooms are excellent choices for the color pink especially if you're doing some kind of therapy with them. In the kitchen, salmon or deep pink is a good color choice. Places that you would not want to use pink are in small spaces like hallways, stairs or alcoves, in the bathroom, home office/study and living room.

Purple is a rich warm color that creates a rich warm space that radiates a feeling of power. Before you decorate with purple, violet or magenta you'll want to make sure that those around you can tolerate it. These colors are not for all people and should be avoided in areas where someone suffers from mental problems, in the kitchen, dining room, home office/study, regular office and the bathroom. These colors are good to use in meditation rooms, sanctuaries, sun rooms, small spaces like entrance halls, stairways, other halls and alcoves, the dining room and living room. You'll still want to use purple, violet and magenta sparingly as they are very powerful and sometimes overwhelming colors.

Blue, Wedgwood, periwinkle, sky and royal blue create relaxation and peacefulness in a room. They make a room look big and airy and give a sense of coolness. When you're decorating a room in blue make sure you include some warm colors through the use of accessories, otherwise the result can be too cold. The best place to use blue in your home is in the bedroom, bathroom, nursery, den or sunroom. For offices, these colors are excellent in any room where you're giving treatment because it helps the patient/client to relax. You want to avoid blues in entertainment areas, halls, stairways and in the dining room. If a room is naturally cold or dark (like a basement) you want to avoid using these colors there as well. Instead you'd choose a warmer color.

Some rooms lend themselves to a combination of both warm and cool colors. An example of this is the home office or study. You need the combination of both colors to motivate you while keeping you relaxed. This enables you to be productive but not overly stressed at the same time.

Turquoise is another color in the blue tones that makes a room look big and airy. It gives the feeling of inspiration to those in it. It's not distracting and will enhance analysis. This is a thinking color. When you are doing something that requires decision making, like working on a business proposal or homework, this is a good color to use. It's also good to use in the bathroom, home office/study, in the bedroom and in small spaces. Because it causes you to think, this is a good contemplative color for a teenager's or tween's bedroom. Try to avoid using turquoise in playrooms though—you'll want warmer, more active colors in there to encourage activity in your children. The dining area is another place where you will want to avoid turquoise. It will limit conversation and have everyone sitting around in deep thought.

Green, including plant shades of green, apple green, mint, sea green and forest green, also makes space seem open and large. The darker the shade, the richer the look. It gives the essence of tranquility and peace to a room, making it seem quiet and undisturbed. This is not the color to use in an activity room or basement but it's great for the bedroom, kitchen, in breakfast nooks or the dining room. You'll also find that greens work very well in natural settings that may include a lot of plants like the patio, porch, sunroom.

Yellow brightens everything. If you use creams, gold and primrose along with all the different shades of yellow you'll find that the rooms in your home are warm, inviting, lively and mentally stimulating. You can add these color variations to any room in your home. You'll want to avoid yellow in the bedroom and should never use it in a bathroom because of its stimulating effect. Yellow is a good choice for aerobics studios, gyms or any business where the clientele needs to be lively and/or mentally stimulated.

Orange, rust and peach are warm colors that give you a friendly and supportive feeling. They are relaxing and aid in digestion so you'll want to use these colors in the kitchen, dining room, living room, rec room, bathroom, hall and in your kid's playroom or in an entertainment area. Try to avoid these colors in your home office/study and in your bedroom. These colors are excellent choices for banks and accountants' offices.

Gold is a wonderful accent color especially during the holidays. It adds a sparkling richness to any color scheme. It is inspiring and joyful.

Silver is another great accent color that adds a touch of class and coolness to spaces. It's a calming accessory color.

Brown is a warm and nurturing color that gives a feeling of safety. It's good for use in floors and as a contrasting color in furniture. The bedroom, living room, dining room and kitchen are ideal for brown as are any other rooms where you will be relaxing. Browns and rich mahogany colors are often used in lawyer's offices because of the safe feeling these colors offer.

Black, in excess, can give off a clinical feel similar to white. It makes spaces look smaller and can make you feel washed out and tired. It can be used in all rooms of the house but it's best used as an accent color to draw attention to other colors. Avoid black in small spaces like halls and stairways or alcoves. Use in moderation or as an accent color in the kitchen and dining room.

White creates a sterile, cool, airy feeling. Too much white and you'll get the clinical hospital effect. It's great as an accent and can be used in all rooms as a contrasting shade.

All tones and hues of gray are neutral. It doesn't cause distraction but instead blends in and highlights other colors. It's kind of blah on its own so it's best used as an accent color. It's also good to only use a little gray in a room because too much of it can lead to feelings of sadness or depression. You'll definitely want to avoid gray if you have someone in your home who has chronic fatigue or clinical depression or if you're decorating a psychologist's office.

Now that you have a good idea of how color can work in your home and office, take a look around and see what changes you can make to open up and energize your living and working space.

Using Color to Energize Your Life

Vitalize Your Personal Presence

We've taken a look at many different aspects of color but now we need to apply those aspects to your daily life. How can you use color to energize your life? Start by experimenting. Do you know what your favorite color is? Or do you like a variety of colors? Do you tend to stick to one or two colors? Or do you love mixing and matching colors in schemes? Whatever your personal style you can change it up and add vitality to your life.

Do you remember when you were in elementary school and the teacher asked you to get out your crayons and color a picture? There's something about coloring that is relaxing and calming, regardless of the colors that you choose. If you haven't colored in a long time, go to your local toy store and buy a coloring book and a big box of crayons. Sit down and color in any way that you want— make the bears blue and the sun green. Be creative and notice all the nuances in color that you choose. This is a fun exercise used to free your mind about any preconceived notions that you may have about color.

Now that you've had some fun and freed your mind, choose one area to work on first. If you've been sick you might want to try color breathing. If you feel that your home is dull and drab then look at the colors you have in your home and consider some redecorating. If you don't feel productive at work then start there. Regardless of the area you choose you're going to do a few things.

First, take stock of the colors currently in use in your wardrobe, home or work place (or whatever area you're choosing). Take notes so you'll have it in black and white in front of you. Second, where can you make changes to add colors that will increase the energy or change the energy? For instance, if you have a red wall in your dining room, do you feel that you're always rushing through dinner or are easily annoyed at the table? Maybe it's time to paint that wall a pale blue or green. If you love the red in the room, then once you've repainted that red wall to a cooler shade then just add a small amount of red as an accent color. Using just a little red will help you tone down the room enough that you'll feel relaxed during your meal while keeping a color that you love. If your spaces feel drab and dull, add color to increase the energy and add vitality. Or if the room is too energetic then add blues and greens to give it a calming effect.

Lastly, you'll take stock in the areas that you've worked on after you've made changes. How does the color affect you now? Did the changes bring balance? If it did then you're on the right track. If it didn't, then make adjustments until you feel that the colors have given you the energy and balance you sought.

Color can boost your personal presence or tone you down if you're coming across too strong. When you're considering color and your personal presentation you should always consider your own coloring first.

Being of Scottish/Irish descent (my maiden name is McDowell), I have fair skin, auburn hair, freckles and hazel eyes that change from green to blue depending on my mood or what I'm wearing. I don't tan, I burn. Scorpio is my sun sign. I find that I'm very comfortable in blues, greens, turquoise, brown, gold, tan and black. For years I wouldn't put on red or orange because of my hair (talk about clashing colors!) but now I will occasionally wear certain shades and tones of these colors that clash less but give me a feeling of power, warmth and vitality. I still have to be careful what hues I select because the clashing bothers me and drains my energy.

Hair color is a big determinate of what others think of you. I couldn't tell you how many times people have mentioned my temper simply because I'm a redhead. And when I tell them I'm a Scorpio I can usually see the "oh crud" expression even though they try to hide it. A redheaded Scorpio? The perception is that redheads have hot tempers and are strong-willed while Scorpios will seek revenge and have a sharp sting. I've actually had people just walk away when they heard that. Talk about rude.

If you have light hair and light eyes then you may also be drawn to blues and greens. If your hair is light and your skin is a darker complexion then you may also prefer rich bright colors. If your complexion is pale then you may like pastels better. Most people consider others who have light hair to be fun loving, outgoing and impulsive.

If your complexion is dark and you have brunette hair, olive skin and brown eyes then you may be drawn to bright, flavorful colors. And you can carry them off well too. That rich bright red that I can never wear, you wear with flair and ease and look amazing in it. With your dark coloring people may think that you're serious, mysterious, sexy and have a vital energy. It is said that people who have darker colored eyes tend to be more outgoing than those with other eye colors.

In what way can someone change their personal presence colors? You can't really do anything about your skin tone even though we may tan or lighten our skin. You can easily do something about your hair though and dyeing your hair is a quick way to make a color change whether you're lightening or darkening it. It's a lot of fun too. I've had my hair strawberry blonde, magenta, nearly black and once I even had a bright purple rat-tail that I wore braided. If you want to make a quick change that will pump up your vitality or change the color schemes that go well with your coloring then change your hair.

Overall, when you use color as a guide, you can create a wardrobe that is vital and energizing while presenting you in a fashionable way that will help you in all that you do in life.

The Color Journal

As you try to bring more color into your life, the best place to start is to find out how much color you are currently utilizing. You also need to determine if your colors are in or out of balance.

Color affects us on many levels—spiritually, emotionally, mentally, psychically and internally—through our auras and chakras. Most people aren't even aware of color. It's like breathing—do you notice each breath you take? No, you don't unless you are focused on the rhythm of your breathing or if you're counting each breath. If you want to become aware of all of the possible ways that color affects you then you have to pay attention. Until you actually start noticing the colors around you, the color choices you make in your daily life and the way you feel about color, then you're not aware of the amounts of different colors you're utilizing.

To keep track of all of the knowledge that you're going to gather about your individual colors I'd highly suggest keeping a journal. You'll want to keep track of the colors you feel drawn to, the colors you wear, the colors in your home and the colors at work. These are examples. You can include as many categories as you'd like to analyze. You'll also want to pay attention to your own body and emotions. Do you have illnesses, aches, pains or areas of concern?

Can you use color to balance both the color in your life and the color within you? You most certainly can if you write it down and track your own personal colors. Try doing the journal for a month. Write in it daily without making comparisons from day to day. Once you've completed a week, look back over that week to see if you can find connections between your emotions, productivity and the colors that you wore or were around that day. At the end of the month, look over all of your entries and find patterns and connections.

To set up your journal, divide it into several sections: wardrobe, work space, home space, ailments and personal preferences. Write down the colors affecting you in each area. Before you go to bed each night, do a quick analysis of your day. How did you feel? Were you productive or did you slack off? Were you anxious or full of energy? The colors around you could be in direct relation to the results of the analysis that you do so don't omit this step.

When you're journaling about your wardrobe write down the colors you wore each day, including undergarments, jewelry and accessories. You'll soon discover patterns in your wardrobe. If you notice that you're wearing the same colors day after day then try to mix it up a little. If you're wearing different colors daily, then try wearing the same colors a couple of times a week. If you notice that on the days you wore red you were very productive but on the days you wore blue or green you just couldn't seem to focus on work then you'll know to wear more red when you need to get things done and blue or green when you've got meetings that require you to be cool and collected.

Use this same process in each section of your journal. Remember to be honest with yourself. If you felt horrible one day make sure you write that down. This journal is for you and if you can't be honest with yourself then who can you be honest with? Journaling is a helpful tool in many ways and keeping a color journal can be very enlightening.

Color and Sun Signs

Everyone knows their astrological sign, also called a sun sign, based on your date of birth. In astrology, your sun sign is influenced by many other factors in the zodiac including your moon sign, rising sign and twelve houses that go together to make up your complete chart. You also consider the elemental qualities associated with your sign and what those mean too. For instance, air signs are good communicators. Fire signs are great leaders that take action. Water signs are sensitive and full of emotion, and earth signs are calm and practical.

Did you know that you also have a color that is associated with your sign? This color relates to the dominant emotions within your sign and is the color that can help heal you when you have health issues or help to strengthen weak body parts. Use the colors associated with your sun sign to help yourself.

Let's take a look at the sun signs of the zodiac to see the specifics. I've listed the colors that many people associate with the zodiac and the ones that I prefer. However, other people may hold a different opinion of the color that is associated with each sign. In this case, I'd say to use the color that feels right to you.

Sun Sign: Aries
Healing Colors: Red
Element: Fire
Emotional Challenges: Impatience, irritability
Problem Health Areas: Headaches

Sun Sign: Taurus
Healing Colors: Blue, Mauve
Element: Earth
Emotional Challenges: Indulgence, laziness
Problem Health Areas: Throat area, neck, thyroid

Sun Sign: Gemini
Healing Colors: Yellow
Element: Air
Emotional Challenges: Can't make decision or commitments
Problem Health Areas: Respiratory system, lungs, chest area, upper arms

Sun Sign: Cancer
Healing Colors: Sea Green, Silver
Element: Water
Emotional Challenges: Insecure, emotional
Problem Health Areas: Breast area

Sun Sign: Leo
Healing Colors: Gold, Orange
Element: Fire
Emotional Challenges: Resentful, withdrawn
Problem Health Areas: Arthritis, back problems, rheumatism

Sun Sign: Virgo
Healing Colors: Navy Blue, Gray
Element: Earth
Emotional Challenges: Critical, inflexible
Problem Health Areas: Digestion, stomach, uterus

Sun Sign: Libra
Healing Colors: Blue, Lavender
Element: Air
Emotional Challenges: Can't make decision or commitments
Problem Health Areas: Kidneys, urinary tract, lower back

Sun Sign: Scorpio
Healing Colors: Crimson, Burgundy
Element: Water
Emotional Challenges: Suppressed emotions, resentful
Problem Health Areas: Sex organs, constipation, intoxication

Sun Sign: Sagittarius
Healing Colors: Purple
Element: Fire
Emotional Challenges: Envy, stress, exhaustion
Problem Health Areas: Thighs, hips, bones, liver

Sun Sign: Capricorn
Healing Colors: Dark Green, Brown
Element: Earth
Emotional Challenges: Responsibility, insecurity
Problem Health Areas: Nerves, skeleton, teeth, skin, tendons of knee

Sun Sign: Aquarius
Healing Colors: Electric Blue, Sky Blue
Element: Air
Emotional Challenges: Too sensitive, dreamy
Problem Health Areas: Hay fever, skin problems, circulation

Sun Sign: Pisces
Healing Colors: Pale Green, Turquoise
Element: Water
Emotional Challenges: Low self-esteem, worrier
Problem Health Areas: Bladder, kidneys, rheumatism, feet

We each have all of the signs of the zodiac within us, with one sign being our predominant one. The color of our sign is the strongest within us but ideally we want to keep all of the colors in balance with one another. You can do this by adding more of the color of the opposite sign that will strengthen your energy while bringing it into balance. If you don't know which sign is opposite yours, I've provided a list here:

Your Sun Sign — Color/Opposite Sign - Color

Aries — Red / Libra — Blue, Lavender
Taurus — Blue, Mauve / Scorpio — Crimson, Burgundy
Gemini — Yellow/ Sagittarius — Purple
Cancer — Sea Green, Silver/ Capricorn — Dark Green, Brown
Leo — Gold, Orange/ Aquarius — Electric Blue, Sky Blue
Virgo — Navy Blue, Gray/ Pisces — Pale Green, Turquoise
Libra — Blue, Lavender/ Aries — Red
Scorpio — Crimson, Burgundy/ Taurus — Blue, Mauve
Sagittarius — Purple/ Gemini — Yellow

Capricorn—Dark Green, Brown/ Cancer—Sea Green, Silver

Aquarius—Electric Blue, Sky Blue/ Leo—Gold, Orange

Pisces—Pale Green, Turquoise/ Virgo—Navy Blue, Gray

The Color Wheel

Quick Reference to Colors

This section is an overview of each of the main colors that we can use to increase our color power. After you've read this book and want to quick reference a color, just flip back here to easily find the information.

Red

Red is a power color. It's high energy and hot. You can use this color to add warmth to a room, add power to your professional appearance and increase your energy levels. It is symbolic of high ambitions, vitality, control, sexuality, passion, loyalty and achievers. It represents vitality and control. Directly related to the circulatory system, it can be used to increase energy levels, enhance or improve sexuality and increase your blood vitality. Problems that can be helped by adding red to yourself and your life are anemia, arthritis, asthma, low or high blood pressure, colds, heartburn and night blindness.

Those who relate to red often demand attention, are high energy, excitable and need to be the center of attention. They strive to be the best at everything, are courageous, extroverted, fun-loving, creative and fiercely loyal. Red can make you act on impulse, keep you moving at a fast pace and help you overcome negativity.

Too much red can lead to aggressive behavior, irritability, impatience and make you quick to anger and cause violent tendencies. It can cause hyperactivity and inconsideration of others' feelings. It can also cause you to feel like a victim or be negative in your approach to life. Red in abundance can cause feelings of mistrust and dislike. It's an indication of illness.

Pink

Pink is a soothing color with calming effects. It nurtures, is unselfish and makes us feel love and protection. It's a romantic color associated with unconditional love. Pink is the most nonaggressive color in the color wheel and it can cause you to feel relaxed and at ease. People associated with pink tend to have high ideals, are modest/shy, gentle, loving and caring. They're good listeners, understanding, compassionate, tend to have their feelings hurt easily and need more support than they reveal.

Pink also eases depression, works well on acne, relieves puffiness and helps breast problems. Too much pink can cause anger, irritability and violent behavior.

Purple

Purple has both warm and cool qualities. It means you feel things deeply, have high ideals and standards and are concerned about things and people around you. Often purple is associated with religion and spirituality, royalty, mystic qualities and clairvoyance. Purple can help you become more open-minded, increase your expectations of yourself and those around you and give you strength.

Purple affects the central nervous system and violet especially helps with arthritis, baldness, bladder problems, gas, rheumatism, scalp problems, tonsillitis, wounds and emotional problems. It also eases the pain of childbirth. Magenta on the other hand is beneficial for brain fogginess, trouble concentrating or any other mental problems.

Magenta is also a good color to use with heart problems.

Too much purple can cause a person to become arrogant or self-serving. You may feel others are trying to make you conform to their beliefs.

Indigo

Indigo is associated with inspiration, spirituality and wisdom. It is a control color and suggests patience and caring. All things are possible with the color indigo. People who are drawn to this color are often animal lovers. Use indigo for allergies, an excessive appetite, croup, dandruff, nosebleeds, migraines, eye problems and skin problems. It is the key color for the nervous system.

Too much indigo can cause you to believe that you're on a higher spiritual plane than other people and you'll start to look down at them.

Blue

Blue is a cool, calming color. You can use blue to make a room more tranquil, calm yourself and project a soothing effect. People who navigate toward blue are creative, imaginative, perceptive, analytical, responsible, highly intelligent, logical thinkers who have a rational outlook on life. They don't often lose their temper, tend not to take risks, are self-reliant, problem solvers, intuitive and probably have psychic abilities. They tend to rely only on themselves but will help others easily. They're full of love, peace, tranquility, affection, tenderness and like quiet places. They feel emotions deeply and tend to be sensitive.

Too much blue lends to a suspicious nature, the inability to trust easily, worry, being overly cautious and loss of control. Obsessive behavior, being a workaholic, fear of failure and carrying too much responsibility are an effect of an excessive amount of blue.

Blue also interchanges with green. It helps toothaches, anxiety, back problems, blisters, high blood pressure, bronchitis, pneumonia, coughs, palpitations, hiccoughs, hoarseness, laryngitis, diarrhea, spasms, nausea, nightmares, pain relief, bleeding, burns, skin problems, respiratory problems and rheumatism.

Turquoise

Turquoise is a cool, calming color. It sends a message of tranquility. It's indicative of sensitivity and creativity, is invigorating but brings calmness at the same time. It's often seen in tropical motifs. People who prefer turquoise are in tune with their feelings, like to talk and have abundant energy. They're organized leaders who are efficient and productive.

Too much turquoise can make you feel despondent, cause you to avoid your true feelings and make it easy for you to get into a rut because you fear change.

It is anti-inflammatory and works to heal earaches and throat problems.

Green

Green is the color of balance, health and happiness. People with green around them are good decision makers with a deep seated calmness, have clear judgment, are observers of life who dislike conflict and seek stress-free situations. They are sensitive, overly cautious, don't trust easily and like to stay in control. They are gentle, soothing, caring, have a solid foundation, even focus and a non-shifting balance. Green promotes healing and rejuvenation.

It stimulates the pituitary gland, regulates circulation and aids the sympathetic nervous system to aid in relaxation by causing us to breathe more slowly and deeply. Green is interchangeable with blue and can also be useful to help anxiety, bleeding, high blood pressure, breast lumps, bruises, burns, chicken pox, concussion, cramps, cysts, diarrhea, obsessions, fevers, hay fever, hiccough, sinusitis, menopause, mumps, strep throat, ulcer, colds and flu.

Too much green can lead toward jealousy, oversensitivity and muddy thinking.

Yellow

Yellow is the color of happiness, activity, spontaneity and fun. Increasing energy, high motivation, risk-taking, facing challenges, overcoming disappointments and conquering conflicts are all accomplished by adding yellow. People who like yellow are idealistic, interesting, have unique ideas, make friends easily, accept responsibility and have minimal stress. They like to stay on the go and have good self-esteem. They are goal setters and risk takers who don't get disappointed easily. Their personalities are outgoing and they seem to radiate joy. Free spirits who love life, they can cheer you up quickly and are compassionate listeners.

Adding yellow to your life can help cheer up your home, give you a positive and happy personal appearance and help ailments such as cramps, abscesses, headaches, appetite loss, gas/burping, constipation, indigestion, stomach ailments, diabetes, kidney, liver or lymphatic problems.

Too much yellow can make you suspicious and untrusting.

Orange

Orange is a warm, happy color that indicates high levels of activity, competitiveness and an ability to take quick action. Orange shows self-motivation, impatience and restlessness. Strong personalities who are dominant and easily frustrated relate to orange. It also is indicative of generous people who are warm with lots of friends that inspire you to be all that you can be and who can lift your spirits without much effort. It inspires creativeness, practicality and a love of life.

Orange can be used to banish low self-esteem, self-pity and obsessive control. It aids in finding forgiveness and releasing grudges. It can help you overcome sadness, depression, abdominal pain, hernias, kidney stones, muscle aches and spleen problems.

Too much orange can cause you to be overly proud and imagine wrongful hurts when none are present. It can cause mental, physical and emotional exhaustion.

Gold

Gold means high ideals, dependability and trustworthiness. People drawn to gold radiate power, they look for the good in every situation, are wise and understanding. They inspire others, are fearless and self-assured. Gold belongs to very spiritual people who enlighten others without even trying. They're usually mentors and guides who are goodhearted and who put their own welfare behind their concern for others. These are balanced individuals with determined focus.

Brown

Brown is an Earth color that shows honesty, sensuality and protectiveness. When people are drawn to brown they tend to hide secrets and seek emotional security. Acceptance is important and isolation is feared. Brown also gives warning of bad moods, a negative outlook and the inability to focus on the positive.

Black

Black suggests being in control. It's also a dire warning of disease or abuse if seen in the aura or energy patterns. Black is masculine, opinionated, controlling, independent and inflexible. Black is used to hide a lack of self-confidence, indecisiveness and the refusal to give up control. Black indicates fear, worry, panic attacks and suggests that you should use caution around people who are drawn to this color. Black can make you feel assertive, daring, independent, mysterious and powerful.

Too much black can lead to depression and feelings of being overpowered.

White

White indicates well-balanced optimism and positive energy. Examples of people associated with white would be a leader whom people look up to or an individual with her own set of unique standards that sets her apart from others. White is the color of change, new opportunity and new direction.

Gray

Gray is a warning sign that indicates illness, depression, loneliness, anemia, low energy levels, tiredness, anxiety and antisocial behavior. People with gray may have a hard time coping with life. Gray also indicates a person who is able to take care of herself, is in control and who has good judgment.

Too much gray can lead to illness, a passive outlook on life, too much work and not enough play time.

Opaque Colors

When observing one's aura you'll notice that you'll be able to see through the colors of energy. If you can't, then this is considered an opaque color. It's very dense and light can't get through it so you can't see through it. When you observe a dense color in an aura or energy field, it shows that the person is struggling with something difficult in her life. She may have unresolved situations that she's trying to work out. This is also a sign of regret.

Transparent or Clear Colors

A transparent or clear color is the opposite of an opaque color because it is easily seen through. Think of looking through tinted glass—the lighter the color the more clear it becomes. When discussing clear colors it doesn't mean they are totally without color but instead the color is easily seen through. When the colors in the person's energy/aura are clear it is indicative of someone who is an open book. They are usually happy, carefree and don't try to hide behind masks or shields. They tend to be wonderful friends who care deeply for others and are loyal to the end. They look at the positives in life—their glass is always half full and never half empty. If you're feeling sad then a person with clear colors in her aura is sure to lift your spirits.

Bibliography

Color Harmony 2 by Bride M. Whelan, Rockport
  Publishers, Inc, Rockport, MA, 1997.
Complete Book of Color, The by Suzy Chiazzari,
  Element Books, Boston, MA, 1999.
Decorating with Color by Donna Sapolin, Hearst
  Books, New York, NY, 1997.
Discover Color Therapy by Helen Graham,
  Ulysses Press, Berkley, CA, 1998.
Energy Secret, The by Jane Alexander, Thorsons,
  Hammersmith, London, 2000.
Healer's Manual, The by Ted Andrews,
  Llewellyn Publications, St. Paul, MN, 1993.
Healing With Color and Light by Theo Gimbel,
  Fireside, New York, NY, 1994.
Homeopathic Color & Sound Remedies by Ambika
  Wauters, Crossing Press, Berkley, CA,
  2007.
Only Astrology Book You'll Ever Need, The by
  Joanna Martine Woolfolk, Stein and Day,
  New York, NY, 1982.

MELISSA ALVAREZ

BIO

Melissa Alvarez is a multi-published, award-winning author who writes nonfiction under her real name and paranormal romantic suspense under the pen name Ariana Dupré. She is also an internationally known clairvoyant advisor and does readings from her site at apsychichaven.com. She owns Friesian horses and German Shepherds with her husband and together they are successful breeders of champions. She enjoys reading and spending time with her family, horses and dogs when she's not writing. Melissa lives in sunny South Florida where the weather is wonderful unless a hurricane is on the horizon. Visit her online at www.MelissaA.com for updates on new releases, contests and a plethora of articles.